Haiku:

Infolded Meaning

One Insight Press

First Edition, 2016
Second Edition, 2026

ISBN 13: 978 – 0692710562
ISBN 10: 0692710562

One Insight Press
San Francisco, CA

My other books can be found here:
https://www.amazon.com/author/dan-brady

Her memorial   this rose
In the folds   meanings
Memories …

Forward

I would like to acknowledge my fourth grade teacher whose name I cannot recall but whose teaching was unforgettable. She engaged us with a wide variety literature and language arts lessons. I learned script writing, performed plays, which we adapted from text, wrote our own stories and poems, which we performed, and we created haiku. It was in her classroom that I first found the fascinating enjoyment of formal writing.
I will also say that writers such as Louis Cuneo and the circle of writers centering on Berkeley's Mother's Hen encouraged my interest in the gentle art of haiku. Louis published my first chapbook "Cast out the Line" a nice selection of haiku.

Many years later I joined the Haiku Poet's of Northern California, a wonderful group of writers, whose meetings are entertaining and illuminating. They have a noteworthy dedication to haiku and I learned a great deal about senryu, haibun and other poetic forms sourced from Japan.

After I began a return to prose, lyric poetry, blank and free verse, I applied what I had learned from haiku to those forms and so it is that haiku influences my style. This book is, in a way, my way of recognizing that influence and to honor the gentle art that is haiku.

As I did in my second book, this volume also contains 3-D text where parenthetical inserts indicate homonyms for the terms they contain - and I encourage giving this book away.

Dan

Introduction

This work demonstrates the range that a haiku has. It is a very limited form, in terms of its structure. Its brevity, 17 syllables, seems restrictive and yet one can, even within such a constraint, successfully write on any of the great themes of literature. One can make one's views known, portray the vital moments of life and death, or speak on love and loss. In the affective realm, the seemingly simple haiku can engender sorrowful tears, emotive sighs, laughter, thoughtful reflections and more just as one can with the other major art forms. Haiku lends itself to infolded meaning where less is more. Despite its brevity, a haiku touches the heart, sparks imagination, insight or prompts intuition to greater considerations. The subtle unfolding, therefore, happens in the mind of the beholder.

These were selected from those written over a 40-year period. Some have been published. Some, when presented, generate the kinds of responses I mentioned above or prompt questions or commentary. I have included personal favorites, some curios or those with merit in the eyes of a close friend. I begin with haiku sourced from my childhood and, overall, proceed to the present. The haiku are organized in sets, some long, some brief and some consisting of individual pieces meant to stand on their own. Some pieces include 3D writing in which parentheses indicate words or homonyms. There are sections of senryu, haiku with a sense of humor. With this book I send all these haiku into the world. You will see, at the end of this book, a suggestion as to how to pass this book along documenting its travels as you do so. As with other books of mine I hope to see this one meet up with me as I proceed along on my walk-of-life.

Table of Contents:

Senryu, 1

Out writing
On a picnic table
Expectant pigeons   edge closer

Oh, what will he do with it?
The ant   crawling all over
The big green grape

Swift   over the pond
The rippled shadow   dragonfly
Low enough   for the frog

Summer pine
Frantic ants struggle— amber
Slowly   takes   its   toll

Luckily,
The crack in my shoe
Admits only water

Pink balloon floats
Along backyards   one by one
Setting dogs to bark

Gold glints on the water
Just
Like it "otter"

Ants come to it   go
Over, around   and all about
The pebble   in their hole

Bond hits –
Into a double play. She, "What's wrong?"
Then he, "Off his meds."

Twenty-nine   thirteen
Fifty-seven   seventy-eight
Haiku!

My Family and I

All those fireflies
Red leaves and   children scatter
Playing   hide and seek

Thank you Mr. Kapp
For giving me a chance   and
Tipping your luck   my way

In the hot shade
Between corn stalks
The pile of sleeping kittens

Tangerine juice
My brother's "sticky hands" caught
That bobbled ball

Loosening my belt
Christmas time with the family
The tree   tilts   goes out

Her sweat for my fever:
Her muscles for my
Diseased, weak bones

That late visit   her
Glance and hesitation   telling
My heart   the news   his death

Dried maple leaf
Pressed in the long unread book
I take its remains

Hair
Just at the temple
She   never   touches

The cat   hops on the table
Walks carefully   through the chess game
Sniffs my nose

Dandelion
     Under his chin
          Remembering childhood

Gold moon on the fence
Setting out the Jack O'Lantern
Then pies   to cool

Water strider
A kick
Ripples   the moon

Charlie and I   high
In the mountains   the horse cloud
Its long   sunset run

Lodge pole pine
Its great roots wrapped around
Blonde riverine granite

None of them saw it
The stone I had skipped
Twenty-five times   or more!

Just stopping to chat
This Veteran's Day
Standing at his grave

Graveside   I look around first
Harmonica for taps
Clear skies at noon

After forty-one years
I ask, "What is the interest
On that $1.37?"

That one time, flowers
At his grave   I never asked
Who   left them

His white tombstone
My cell phone thrums on and on
His nephew calling

The TV, the phone rings
Then, the doorbell – it all adds up
Cold toast

Seventy million years old
The fossil shell on the mantle
In candle's light

All day long
My big toe   through this sock's hole
Reminded me

Inside my left shoe
The cold spot   quickly dampens
One step at a time

All the cool spots
In my favorite plaid
Blustery March day

Washing his wool cap
For the first time   since it was mine
My h(airs) t(here) too

In the mirror
Seeing mom's smile   in mine
Thinking back   that last time

Heartache continual
At night   it presses on
Each breath   mom's reminder

Michigan road trip
Reminiscing past corn
And more damned corn

Her phone call
She brings up the cancer
Letting me ... off the hook

In Jim's kitchen –
Making each other laugh so hard
To see who'll fall over

Gaggle of giggling girls
So what else would you expect?
Family reunion

To hot to handle
Or to think of eating it
Smelling   the pizza

Summer noon   he naps
On the veranda   scattered newspapers
Slowly   flap

Riverside
Rough campfire   talking story
We, Braveheart's men, laugh

The great blue heron
Wades out   upstream of us   so
We stop to cast

Good   cold water
Poured down   feeling it in the belly
Thirsty

Summer   orchard
Throwing apples at the old tree house
Laughing myself silly

Gray at his temple
Not forgetting   one tear brims
Killing field story

Soft warm sunlight
Counting 100 breaths   not so easy
As one might think

This recent photo
Does nothing but injustice
Why even smile?

At the open mic
Having a real good laugh
At my own expense

Sleeping in like a champ
Touching floorboards at 2pm
Breakfast   at 3

THOMAS G
BRADY
NEW YORK
SGT
SCOUT DOG PLT
VIETNAM

We, two

> *Wedding night*
> *As we undress   birdseed scatters   all over*
> *The tiled floor*

> *Sweet embraceable you*
> *Light on our (feet)   we trip with time*
> *Word up baby   word!*

> *Her sweet kiss*
> *Given on the play ground's swings*
> *Teenagers again   still*

> *Clothes tossed on the chair*
> *Laughing at their chance embrace*
> *We go for a hug*

In the plastic turquoise tub
Her entangled bras ...
Adrift

Your scent ... my whisper
At your ear ... cheek to cheek ...
Eyes closed ... with your smile

On our small green rug
How many ways CAN we hop off?
We'll get back to you

As I set the receiver
Into its cradle   that sound –
Did   she wire me a smooch?

She gave me raspberry kisses
In the kitchen
Oh   yes she did   sweet

Our candles steady flame
Reflected in the pane   outside trees
Wildly buck and sway

She laughs – so I laugh
I know she's found the heart –
And now   she's hiding it

She walks through
Low hanging drifts of incense
Wisps   drawn   after her

On the phone, worlds apart
You say, "It's the same moon."
As I touch the cold (pane)

Spring   our hillside
We lay back ... watching sunset
Laugh at cloud shapes

We two, the holidays

Our old ornaments
As we take them out again
Telling their stories

Our " first" ornament
Cracked   set on each year with
Tradition and fare

Pine needle shadows
Spread   over the ceiling
In a rainbow's glow

Chilling wind outside
Her holiday mail   heavier
Than the fruitcake

Her hands shake
Dropping the letter – faded photo
Her new   old tears

All that day   cold wind
This sand dollar   incomplete
Will always be ours

As she talks   behind her
Outside the window   a spider
Racing to its victim

New Years
Amid confetti   on the sidewalk
Her broken tears

Rainfall at our feet
This old year passes away
New shoes   stepping out!

Midnight   his shadow slips
Off the curb   across the street
Into the edge of night

Beneath the door knob
Arcing strokes cut the finish
Crossing the grain

March   Christmas tree
In full trim   under all those needles
A sheet   for snow

Dawn ... at low tide
She smiles   the sound from the shell
Held to her ear

Hearth and home

Living room plants
Turning them again
Winter solstice

Blustery winter night
From the bag of pomegranates
A cautious snail

Rain tapping the sill
As I pull the shade   low
My elbow creaks   loud

"One more time," he says.
"Just try it," she says coldly.
And don't roll your eyes!"

Sharpening the blade
Running my tongue   along its edge
Tangy taste   blood and steel

New Moon's night
Beyond the wall   in pitched shade
Wind chimes'   slight serenade

After the night's rain
Blown leaves stuck to the window
Dawn's colorful collage

Crossing the room
His footfalls rebound inside her cup
So   tea leaves settle

Why is it always
Something or other   just as
I   want   to sit down

Rosemary and sage
Hung to dry in the window
Blue flowers on the sill

Coat catching   the branch
Released   springs back
"A cold shower," he laughs!

Not even spinning –
A white petal   still enters
The study window

The breeze is up
Blossoms flutter
Writing invitations

The phone jangles
Summer lightning   close!
I pick up the dead line

S.F heat wave
Mid 80's   all day long
The unmade bed   stays that way

Teaching: students and children

— Haiku hikes: McLaren Park

May   kids off the hook
Into grassy meadows
Making dandelion wishes

Big yellow rose
Children gather close   to smell
A bumping of heads

Paying them no mind
Gopher   pushing out soil
As children chatter

Girls giggle
As the gobbled gopher
Wriggles in the heron's neck

Children chase them
Dragonflies change altitude   hover
Above outstretched hands

Out in the pond
One rock   catches their eyes
Before it hops   under

— Haiku from school

They try their hand
Show me their world in smiling pictures
Of everything

The shuffling of feet
And snuffling of noses
Spring breeze through the classroom

First real spring rain
Children burst out of the room
Smiling to the sky

New playground's blank black
In the huge puddle   bright clouds
Hiding the sun

Recess on the yard
The children loudly playing
All their made up games

Children run up to me
Smiling laughing and   silly
How bright their eyes are

Near the hopscotch game
Last day of school   ice cream puddle
Captures a paper airplane

The child I once knew
First boyfriend in one hand
A basketball   in the other

Hot   still   July
Listless teacher's conference   outside
For all to hear   ardent doves   coo

The teacher   walking
Passes cardboard boxes, says,
"Those aren't in bad shape."

Gardening and back yards

Easter lily
Its golden pistil   flocked with pollen
Sparkled with dew

Tying a blackberry
To the poles   using grass stems
Weeded from the garden

Too late!   the sun's glint
On the web's anchor strand
Catching over my face!

In the cleft of clover
Single dewdrop gleams
All the sun's circle inside

Black bumblebee
Ambling on the zucchini's bloom
Tumbles inside

Motionless bee
On the large ripe strawberry
Picking its neighbor

Rosemary blossoms
Bees in and around them
No time for a trim

How I do weeding:
Dig them up carefully
Replant in the "wild zone"

Pulling up onions
A shard of blue china
Shows up as well

Compost turned
Insects in disarray   they scatter
At every move I make

A down feather caught
On a ripening tomato's crown
All week long

Those hunting spiders
Between the chard and squash
No earwigs last night

Twisted   the broken
Plum bough   hangs down
Covered in blossoms!

Flapping jay settles
Onto the old lemon's branch
Grabs the big wriggler

A sparrow hops about
On stepping stones
I hem and haw   over teas

Those unnamed flowers
Outside my garden   visited by bees
Just the same

Innermost folds of the rose
The dew pearls   within
Tuesday's noon siren

A single leaf
Clearly singing
How   can this be heard?

The head of the rose
Cut
The stem quivers

That morning   crows
Seven   raise such a ruckus
We meet back yard neighbors

June   nesting ringnecks
Put off six crows   aerial combat
All afternoon

The garden gate
Open   in the moonlight
A web's   glistening array

By the garden path
The moonlit wildflowers
Move   as I remain   still

In the bowl   long left out
Full of rain   over settled leaves
The moon and stars

Senryu, 2

Ungodly snoring
His alarm clock   going off
Finally   at dawn's light

Philosophy: underwear
On the floor   makes everything
Fruit of the Loom

Men in the next booth
Over steak, chili, eggs and coffee
Complaining about gas

Three girls   klatch
Texts on fertilizer
With the horrid waft   they laugh

Medical student
Anesthesiology book
As a pillow

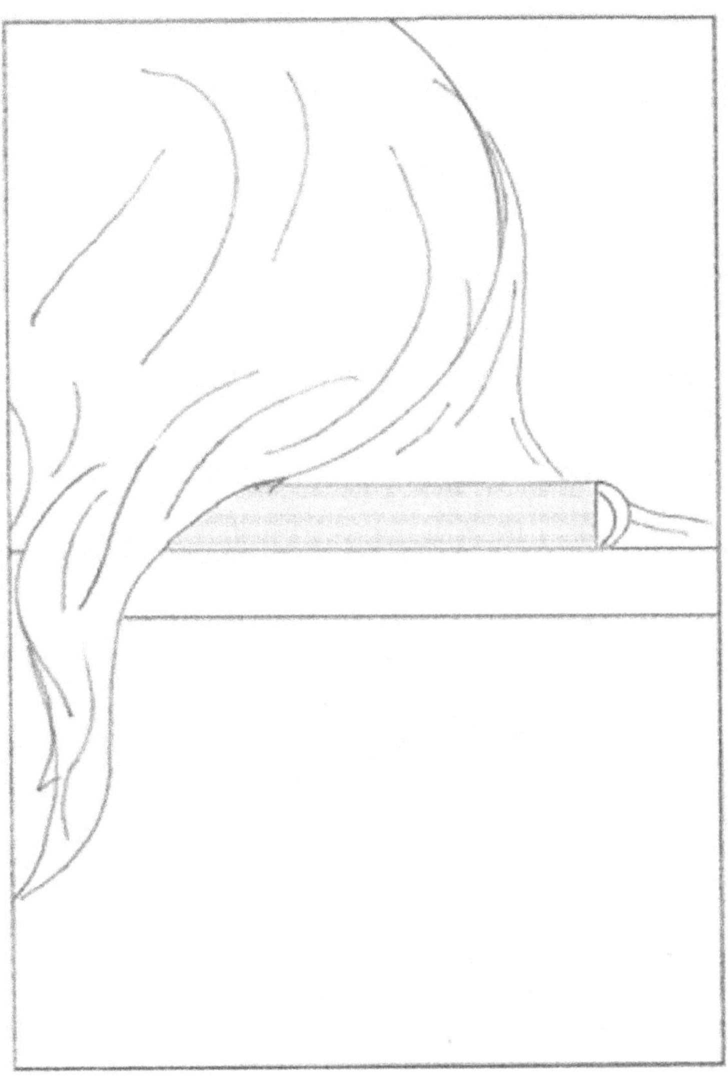

Parks

Old picnic table
Splatters of lichen and moss
Grow into its engraved checkerboard

Preeners and strutters
Pitching "coo," they're "in the mood"
Between pecks for food

Pigeon's world
On the asphalt by the pond
They all got it "going on"

At the park   wind
Takes an empty baby carriage
Out for a ride

Starlings on monkey bars
Approaching toddler   falls "splat"
They scatter   up and away

Finally   ceasing my nap
On the cool, green shady park bench
Too many passers by!

Rusty rebar bent
Inside the old bunker
With a view of the bridge

Lucent new grass
In the dark gravel around
The rusted out hatch

Eucalyptus seeds
Over the pathway   each step
Crunchy   pungent

Reflections in puddles
Far beneath my stride
Birds in flight   where clouds abide

Magnolia bloom
Pristine   fallen onto mud
The bee finding it

Elderly man jogs
Barely in form   stops nearby
Smiles into the breeze

On its own bed
Of broken limbs tangled branch and roots
The giant redwood   at rest

Stones in the creek
Do they carry the echo
Of my hiking song?

Butterfly   beating hard
Up wind   and the path
Sidestepping it

Hikers on the trail
About a half mile away
Their talk   on the breeze

Above the footpath
Cresting the hill   butterflies crisscross
Ahead of Mount Diablo

Near the yarrow
Where paths converge   several
Mission Blue butterflies

June   high noon
Between table planks – in the cobweb
One glistening dewdrop

He hits   breaking the bat
Oh   but the crowd   cheers
Yet   he just makes first!

A pop fly
They go wild but   it's   caught
This batter   slowly returns

The ball players   gone
Robins take to the infield
Hunt and peck   around

He takes her
Onto the pitcher's mound   points here   there
Explains the empty field

Out by third
Two children laugh   kicking
At their big red ball

Swept up   whirling
Leaves, shreds   dust and down
Their shadows circle   'round

Spring zephyr
Cherry blossoms   settle
On the Buddha's palm

(Their) sprinkling on the moss
Pearlescent dewdrops   reflect
A brightening overcast

Bright   clear   New Year's Day
Their breath clouds mingle
As they kiss, laugh and walk away

Land's End in fog
My tree fades
As did the world before it

Ponds

Cast   the line
Hook   again
The quiet

Blue August sky
Reflected in the pond   when   something
Ripples it all

On algae clumps
Where my shadow came to stay
Mosquito fish school away

Six ducklings   nearing shore
Mother swiftly cuts them off
A stroller's approach

Dazzling damsels
Red and blue   joined in flight
One shadow on granite

A koi's tail
Brushing the surface   trace
Of ripples   swirled

The old gardener
Trims a tree   leaves fall to the pond
Three great koi   pause

Summer rain   sprinkles
Across the pond   dissolving trees
Clouds   all the heavens

As drops start to fall
The fleet of ducks – turn as one
Make for shore

Animals

Plop!   on my paper
The tiny grasshopper   sets
Just long enough and   goes

Slashing a line
Across the page   a tiny insect
Dies   in the stroke!

The ant   wanders
Amid the numbers and shadows
Of the sundial

Sunlit, tall summer grasses
A grouping of poppies
A'sway with bees

Dragonfly's shadow
On the hot August sidewalk
(you're) words worth

The egret stands   reflecting
For hours
The distant shore   its busy highway

Honeysuckle tangles
The wagon wheel spokes
On iron rims   snail tracks

The leafless plum
Jays settle   bowing their branch
Breaks   they fly off   calling

Winter's light
Upon the downy bobbing bottoms
Of upended ducks!

In the sky
A flight of herons
Long   your auburn hair   remembered

The old gray parrot
Caged   its searching eye
On a butterfly

Thrumming cicadas
In the dark   elusive rhythms
Move   time   and space

Clematis tendril
Points out   a grand old moon
Here   and there   cricket

The wind   the rain
This wet sidewalk   snail   you?
Out on a night like this?

Doe and fawn
The mother drinks from the lake
Rings   on and   on

Ocean Beach

> *Headlands   fade in haze*
> *Morning joggers near the surf*
> *Their hound bounds into waves*

> *In the dunes   sneakers*
> *Socks neatly tucked in   and*
> *Grass growing out their tops*

> *On the pier   drawn along*
> *With the water's   ebb and flow*
> *Motionless   motions*

> *Chill November wind*
> *Sweeps just over the sand*
> *Uncovers   tattered moth wings*

The tide turns
A wave sweeps   my track
All those steps   washed away

A duck   a wreck
In a wrack   crab legs   shells
Drift wood   clouds of flies

The soggy looped neck
Of the cormorant   belly split
Cupping water

Less than a pool
More of a puddle   its hermit crab
Scrappy enough

*Fog swirls about
The beach   disappears
Only the sand at my feet*

*Tall   single grass stem
Gone to seed   rooted
In a boulder's   slight fracture*

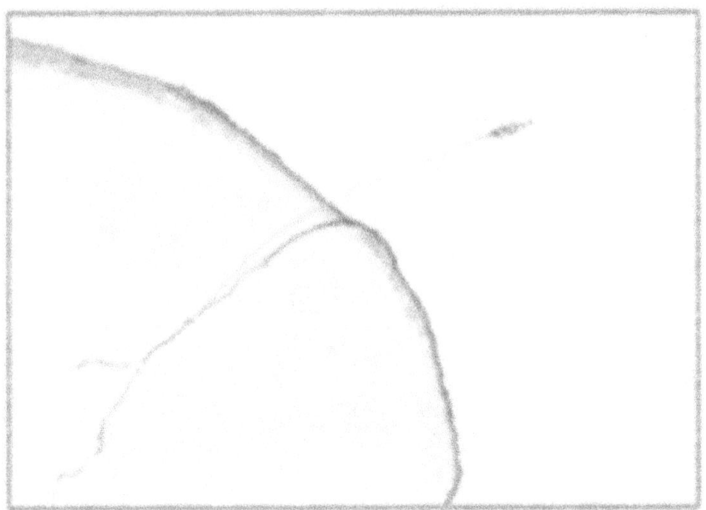

Beach Bonfires

That moment
Winter's solstice sun   winks out
Chill gusts   whip   snap

With the first match
Our pyre   goes up quick
One by one   we step back

Setting crescent moon
Seen through climbing flames
Wavering   as we sing

Ocean Beach
Dusky horizon   pelican silhouettes
Under the first star

Strangers drawn to it
The crackling blaze on the beach
The sand steams

Ocean Beach   waning fire
Homeless man   stops to sit in
Shows us his fishing gear

A new log tossed on
Sparks billow   roiling up
To mingle with the stars

Coals radiant white
Gusty winds pulsing their hues
Wood grain   lines of night

For the longest time
The blazing chunk of wood
Has eyes   nostrils

Wind shifts seaward
Fans coals and ash by the log
Reigniting the fire

Preservation Hall at Stern Grove

Applause for
The first umbrella dancer   down front
In a sudden shaft of light

"Georgia On My Mind"
Couples form in the aisles
Slow dance it   old style

Bubble passing him by
The trombone player
Swirls one 'round his slide

Basin Street Blues
We all wave pink pages   in time
Bubbles above us all

Picnic   two toddlers
On their gingham field   dance
To Gershwin's jazz

The old bench of stone
Deliciously warm   all day
I nod   in and out

Barefooted
The toddler onto spring grass
Giggles with each step

Toddler kicks so hard
His shoe   goes farther than the ball
Dad cries, "Fair shoe!"

Travels

Oregon   August
All day long   dandelions
Blow over the road

Corvallis   summer
Downtown a Toshiba office printer
Now a sidewalk planter

Dappled shadows shift
Two lively river otters
Forever cast in bronze

Unpleasantly hot
Unseen visitor   jasmine
Goes with me a ways

Before hazy pines
Myriads   billow and flow
All backlit   aglow

Rolling fields of stubble
Hawks atop the nearby oaks
Vultures   on thermals

In this field
Going wild
Idle tractor

Their flight   over the field
A murder of crows   turn slowly
To circle above me

All day   one cricket
Over the field   at dusk
One more   joins in

Waxing full moon sets
Old barn   makes odd noises
Every few minutes

The melon cooling
In the shallow stream
Summer evening's moonrise

All day long   two pals
Work together   surprised when told
Of their twin shirts

Up in the loft
They play intense chess
Mars in their window

Blue   under blue haze
Lake Tahoe in the distance
From the windy pass

Ripples on the pond
Somewhere   in tule fog
A loose canoe   bumps and grinds

The grey heron
On the rip-rap   there   all along
Surprising second graders

Utah rest stop   the car
Wide open   on the steering wheel
Grey moth   takes a break

Purple lupines
Over miles of rolling hills
Lost in South Dakota

Two AM
At the long, long   red light
A flurry of leaves passing through

Kit Carson's gravesite
Wrought iron fence and gate
Its new lock   rusted

Motel mirror
The bright white light shows each flaw
Tears and more tears

Stock bar conversation
LA; brisk autumn
Banker   bowler   and beer

Tidy gentleman
Runs with the wind   calling
After his flying letters

Filmy blouse   backlit
The curving silhouette
A (peak)   no bra

Early morning   spring
Here   amid apple trees
The Mission bells' alleluias

Thick rough swollen
Her hands   hold small blue flowers
All her wrinkles   smile

Winter sunset   nuns
Walk along   preceded
By their long   long shadows

Homeward bound
Cold steel handrails   on childhood's bridge
Broken childhood tears

January night
Raindrops   tap the snare drum
Doing a number on its head

Frosted windowpanes
We draw holiday greetings
With hearts and angels

Winter night clear
The day's heavy snow   in drifts
Orion rises

Snowdrift landscape
Teakettle's hush   low winter's dawn
All day long   I yawn

Under this heavy snow
The compost pile
Vents

Worn stretched denim
Tight over my knee   I feel
The ambling fly

—A Wedding

Floral knots   and ribbons
The "party car" I pass by
Going to your wedding

A great oak's shade
One dandelion seed   drifts
Appearing   disappearing

A sudden shaft of light,
The bride's hair and gown— aglow
"Reverent" on his lips

At the reception
Single girls   dance the first tune
Men   standing by   watch

Raucous laughter
From the circle of young men
Toasting and boasting

Their champagne glasses
On brickwork   dancers just miss them
Again and again

My carrot cake
A blue petal   falls onto its frosting
I eat it too

Lemon iced tea   nice
The girls   chat on about the ages
As if they had time

His mother's gesture
Sweeping   the glass falls – shatters
To laughter   and applause

All Bay Area Sufi Camp

Pine tree campground
In the deep dusty tire's track
A toddler's footprints

We clear off branches
Stomp around to put down loam
Making our tent's space

Sleeping outside
I wake up   over and over
Because of that one rock

Opening prayer
He leads the invocation
A gold fly   set at his lip

Heart of the circle   vacant
Save for its   instruments
Resonant   with singing

The graying man
Alongside the rickety fence
And that old pond   at noon

Glances in dances
What matters is what chance is
Insignificance

What he said
Just before the startling gong
Much funnier with it

As she speaks of men
And women— dust motes swirl
With her every gesture

Branches sway   with breeze
Her child on her hip   she moves
Modeling the two step

Nothing like it
Dozing   as mild zephyrs play
And   dancers sing

Falling leaves   twirl
Flicker in noon light   confuse
This butterfly's flight

Not a breath of wind
The plum blossom's fragrance
Only in the shade

Having snapped it
The banana slug   crawls
Over a broken twig

Fallen redwood   roots   up
Tangled in clumps of earth
New shoots   from its trunk

Two long shoots from a stump
In the webbing between
Several wrigglers

Up this dry stream's bed
Black and white butterflies
One   after the other

Over the boulder
Oak leaf shadows   slip
Into dusty gloom

Monoplane's drone
As the fly wavers up the trail
Below my (feet)

Ants' busy route
Across the boulder   wending
Twigs, lichen and leaves

Sequoia   burnt out   hollow
In a circle of sky   clouds move
She sways slightly

Spring wind rushes
The whorls of my ears   each glance
Pitches the sound!

Up the glen   the warm draft
Carries hapless mosquitoes
Away from campground

Bob blows the wildebeest horn.
I clang Tibetan bells.
Then we howl as hounds!

In the woods   birdsongs
From the kitchen   pots and pans
Avalanche   and shouts

Dining hall
Passing islands of conversation, he says,
"Beats channel surfing."

Zikr in the hall
In the silence after
We sigh with the breeze

L(a)te fire   music
((s(h(a))(ring)) (((am)((u)se)((men)t))
telling, j(ok)es a circle of friends

Speaking in "tongues"
We confound the youngsters
Who ought to know better than listen!

No water   we conspire
To piss out the fire
Rude jokes meet worse verse

Still pond
In reflection   fireflies
Circle the moon

Crickets stop
At my approach   begin again
Behind me

Glancing back
The star's faint reflection
In the pond   disappears

Lunch   we all
Give away treats, tell tales and jokes
As if there were no tomorrow

So, he naps
As branches motion   flurries of leaves fall
Settling on him

Volleyball in the pool
Time passes us by   the score?
Love All

At Lama Foundation

Birds building their nest
In the rain gutter   all day long
Storm clouds   to the west

Airy   cumulous mountain
Drifts   its sunny limb brightens
Warmth   yet to come

Hail in August
Bounces into the sauna
Waiting it out

After the rain burst
The hard packed path   steaming
Changes color

Yellow butterflies
Circle one another   the gust
Carries them off   away   separated

At Sam's maqbarra
Plants sprout between its white stones
I cry anyway

Touching the heart stone
I see   many gifts   sprinkled
From head to foot

Dusk   at the summit
Counting   seven horizons
The farthest one   pink

Westering sun
From the clouds brilliant fringe   beams
Spokes of a wheel

Three black ants   struggle
Moving the wasp along the path
So   I step over

New Moon's night
From a canopy of shadowy gloom
Petals   from an unseen bloom

Summer evening
Doors open   utensils clanging
Then we get the breeze

Arc of the heavens
Milky Way   so clear
Breeze   shifting plants   near

Kirtan from the dome
Cat Stevens   from the kitchen
Mixing   on the steps

As he begins
To strike his Tibetan drum
Quiet   distant lightning

Again and again
Butting against the huge window
The great moth at sunset

Day after day
Large black spider   circumambulates
In the kiva

Each step   is another
Toward the last   my reflection grows
In the large window

Staying cool
I shift my chair with the tree's shadow
All afternoon

The leaf,
        Caught up for a moment,
      Falls.

Blackbird puffs out
  Each note moves its tail   the reed perch
    And   their shadows

Closed   the roses sway
The spaces   between their stems
Changing   shape

Butterfly shadows
Crossing the mudflat   flutter
In and out of cracks

Black mare at the trough
Drinking   insects   up in the air
About it

Taking this cicada
Out of the deep sink   pity
For its lost limb

Frying pans and pots
Clatter into collapse
Conversation chatter starter

Kitchen garden
Under spinach leaves   on a cool rock
Sleeping black kitten

Inevitably
Oatmeal   fruit and honey
Sunrise breakfast

Between pitchers
A pinecone's loosed seeds
Decorate a white tablecloth

Guests   at the buffet
Chat   load up their plates   below
Cat   crunching its mouse

Spring sunlight
Kids' clothes   dance on the line
Roses bob beyond

Adobe bricks   set up
Course after course   we work
Until the mud fight

In the shade
Feet chill in the stream   a few steps off
Hot summer waits

Drum circle at the pyre
Above the ridge's silhouette
The galactic arch

Urban Grit

Clement Street's letters
Worn down   deformed
Fallen into exposed gravel

Gentle autumn rain
Shoe print mud puddles at the curb
School bus stop

Geary Street sidewalk
Hidden in the very small tree
Two bickering birds

Baseball cards   scattered
On the sidewalk, face up, in the rain
Their beautiful finish

Frail old woman dressed in black
Gingerly steps through them

Sidewalk impression
Sneaker print's   verdant patina
Highlights circlets

Near gum's foil
The splatter   a hatchling   its large round eyes
Closed   soft

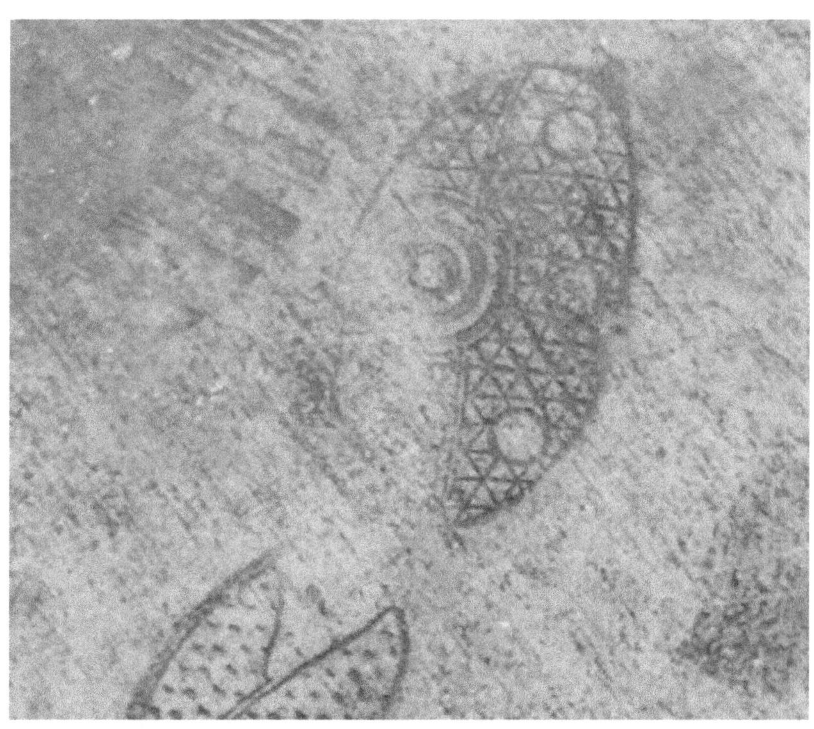

Inside Pizza Hut
Six pink haired ladies chat   laugh
Scratching   their tickets

This window washer
Passes by   spits on the sidewalk
Picks his nose   flicks it

Afternoon   dusty sidewalk
With each step   grit grinds
Drops of sweat move

Summer   hot asphalt
The yellow caterpillar
Undulates in haste

Standing just outside
A "Hall of Fame" at the curb
Dozens of dead rodents

Mission curbside
Lots of Corona caps
Then   the lone Budweiser

Pick up B-Ball
Dudes in their T-shirts hoot and holla
Each shot goes with anothu' t'follah'

Her exhaled smoke
Reveals a shaft of light   and
Spider web shadows

Sidewalk waffle boot print
Thick brown liquid   last night's beer
Its smell   all to clear

Toward each other
The cane   its reflection
In a puddle's perfect plane

Rose petals
    On dingy damp granite   on the breeze
        Cigarettes   urine

Doorway   homeless huddled
Inside twin porcelain Dalmatians
Look on them

Oh   the wind outside
And the rain   the sake cools
Men behind us   laugh and laugh!

Moonless   summer night
Open window   the stroller's whistling
Staggers with him

Long after midnight
In the vast office   one phone
Rings   on and on

Loomis at Barneveld
Midnight   the balloon drifts along
Dragging its string

A bit of breeze   gives it a lift
It follows   for some time

Dawn   Civic Center
The drunk passed out   still gulls stand by him
One bright star

Sun bright
My lucky dime falls
Rings   around   wet black asphalt

Broken umbrellas
Swept along Market Street
MUNI lines down   signals on the blink

On the bank's red brick steps
One dark silk stocking   draped,
Rain soaked and dripping

Cold autumn morning
Lame pigeon limps along
Among skyscrapers

Fluffed and tucked up
Grounded at the bank's façade
Ill   aged pigeon

In the tenderloin
Flapping along in chill winter breeze
Pink Valentine's heart

Sutter at Fillmore
Overcast   drizzle   steaming cup
Left on the news rack

Through Burger King's (pane)
He has black coffee   a smoke
A rheumy-eyed   stare

In gutter water
Some french-fries with their flowing
Rainbow oil slicks

Pigeons disturb
The chicken bones   near the tire
Turned to the curb

Doughnut shop   the men
Speak Chinese   smoke   chat   yell
And cough New Year's Day

Powell at Market   spring night
Blues band   wails   plays it tight
Sax solo   waaaaay   all right!

Loud alcoholic
Blathers on   winter light glares his glasses
Hiding   his eyes

Market Street
Chess for money   he slaps it down
Double sacrifice   forced mate!

Coffee   doughnut
His table   a concrete trash bin
Laid with blue silk

Good old Mary
Gray haired   but sharp   blue eyed
Dishing out advice   with coffee

Downtown alley   grungy door ajar
On its new green welcome mat
Hypodermics

Mission Street's flower girl
Offers the same kind
As at Mom's memorial

For dance or dating
The single shoes on display
With lively music

At the corner
The wealth of the produce stand
The homeless man's rig

Two men try to talk
At 24th and Mission
Traffic frustrates them

Ant touching
The blue ale cap   with feelers
Going round and round

Early morning
Old woman   scrapes spring growth
From her sidewalk's crack

Senryu, 3

Half an hour
Obese boy waits for MUNI
Gets off two stops later

Handwritten sign
On the red Ferrari for sale
Illegible details

Bullet hole decals
On the 67 ford
Being restored ...

Lightning
Then   its thunder   the ants
Speed it up

Yes, my beard is gray;
My skin wrinkled but darling—
It's that moon   again!

Politics?

> *Topsy-turvy*
> *Richard Nixon's stamp   crooked*
> *And cancelled out*

> *Protest!*
> *Doesn't get any footage*
> *At the Super Bowl, see BS*

> *"… but no TV at home …"*
> *The profound, nay pregnant pause,*
> *After that clause*

> *"Howard Stern," he said,*
> *"a snotgobbling, foppish cynical brat*
> *Or heathen parasite."*

Above ground zero
Years after those towers burned
Gulls fly   unconcerned

Making a point of it
That suffering dimbulb   usually called
The global village idiot!

Bush:
Unadulterated asshole,
Or not – that's the question!

Lower and lower
The rice in the jar   winter
Job loss headlines

Spring   lace curtains   arc
Over wooden chessman
Toppling the king   onto stone

Military graves
Crows move out   hunt all over
The quiet   remains

September twilight
Our flag   hanging at its pole
Is not bestirred

Worst-case scenario
The world given over to lesser Gods
All known by name

Somewhere in Iraq
A woman moans   as she dies
Along with this moon

Abu Ghraib autopsy
Crushed larynx   blunt force trauma
Homicide

Krauthammer's phlegm:
To preserve our values   we
Must abandon them

Coring them out
Purple sprouts   from the red potato
Afghanistan's news

More and more
Things have stopped making sense
So grows my indifference

Interrogation:
What causes heart attacks
In twenty-somethings?

Gaza   dynamite
At their hearts   splattering
Thoughts and argument

Are there cures
For the hardened hearts   cold eyes
And numb minds, which measure pain?

What happens to him
He who flips the switch   gouges
Beats   or water boards?

Extraordinary
Rendition   take it apart
Find tears   hidden screams

How to Kowtow
Lesson one: if an American, apologize
Offer your neck

That dollar thirty-seven
The change in his pocket
That   last day   Vietnam

What is the interest?
What   the principle?

Arizona
Mothballed bombes   on a prop up high
Blue butterfly

Tank turret
Between its handholds
A spider's web

— *Ecological Issues*

> *The egret   lifts   afternoon*
> *On the salt marsh   surveyors*
> *Wave   one to the other*

> *In blue grey earth*
> *Grain stalks   both drawn and dry*
> *Nothing   but the crop*

> *Torn earth   broken cement*
> *Before me   here and now*
> *And all around the world*

> *Please stop buying*
> *Anything made of plastic*
> *I mean really*

"Planned obsolescence:
A system of self-destructive
Automatic defaults"

Greenpeace mailing   saved
Its full blank side
Useful for notes

— First Nations

Arizona ruins
Among some pottery shards
Kernels of black corn

Unnamed   unnumbered
On hallowed ground   here   yet
The Mission's Indians

Even here
That Arizona burial ground
Is not quiet

— The long term

Armageddon   comes in
On
Little   cat   feet

Building a planet?
Just possibly easier
Than fixing this mess

This world's ending
Not so much a concern
Compared to what comes next

World recipe:
Start with nickel-iron
Bring to a boil – add ice as needed

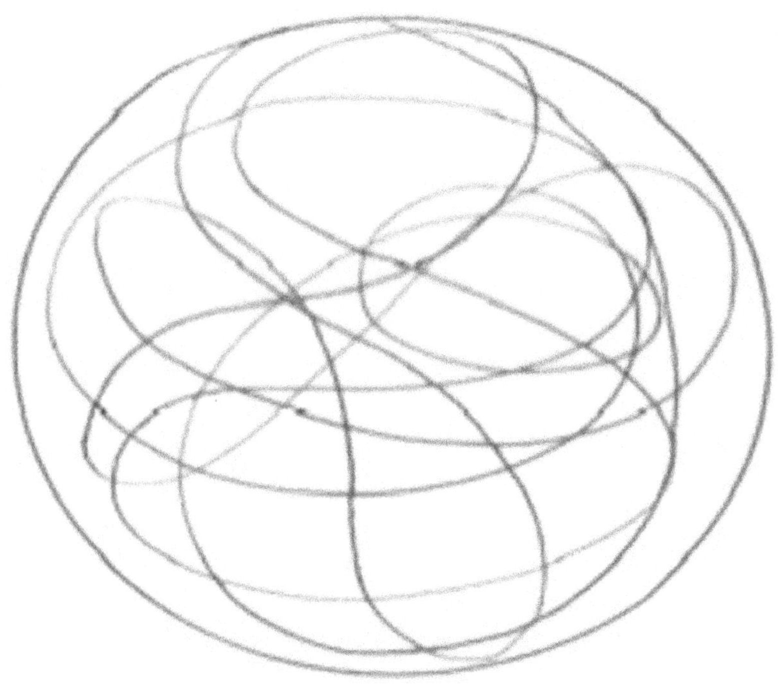

Philosophy

They talked about
What's universal or not
He said, "Nothing's universal."

There are   almost
No
Absolutes

Zen   in reality
Is
Nothing at all

Zen riddle:
How far can you travel – when
One step takes you everywhere?

Really little
Except only smaller
The Zen master   is

Which do you prefer
Your nose   or the rose? Question:
What's the difference?

Formally speaking
All I hold against religion
Are its trappings

That which is m(o)st
In the eggs way   is
The egg's ((weigh))

Christ's syllogism:
"If to thine own self be true, then
Heal thyself, physician."

Render unto Caesar
That which is his!   Just what is?
Nothing at all!

Hold on   Hold on!
Until is yanked off
The flesh

Hajj – when inside
With the Kabbah   circle face out
"Polish the mirror"

A word of s(ea.)son
Is ((nat(ur)(all)y) ((p(re.)sent))
((un(o)(b)serv(ed.))); (q((u)i)e.t.)

s((o)ver))eign e(ye)
(r(ad)((I))(a)nce) bobbing water
the bro(k(e)n) birdbath

Senryu, 4

In the choir
After chocolate rabbits
We all hit the low notes

With a cam(o)(u)flage shirt
He says, "(no) one sees me
For w(ha)t I am!"

Men   at least
Can pee into sinks   water running
Saving the Earth

Unintelligible
Her vodka whisper   not so
Her wandering hands

Well, a cigarette
Smashed out   in the guacamole
The morning after

I sit as the thinker
Unlike him   figuring
Why I came in here ...

On the fresh laundry
Of course   the cat chooses this
Neat pile   for its nap

Letting the old toaster go
Explanations   details
And   misdirection

The slow fat goose
Giving me the eye
As I take a gander

On dry grass
What with all his ruffle necking
She flies the coop!

Death

Lightning   flickers
My face   in the rain-streaked pane
But darkly

Balloon on the floor
Idly kicked by those few
Remaining   New Year's

Sidewalk puddle
Snowflakes   and their reflections
Vanish together

May freshet sounds
Dogwood petals flutter
Toward an open grave

Old couple   tossing coins
In the fountain   ripples reflected
On their faces

Baby comforter
Shaken out   given the once over
Mom's last moving day

Crooked headstones
Tall summer grass gone to seed
The bursting covey

With Tom, light spring mist
Droplets collect   to run down
The lines of his name

Her folded fingers
Over the mug of hot tea
Steam through their uneven gaps

Empty white china bowl
Old woman   her daughter staring
At their hands

Tossing ashes up
In his finery of dust
Sunbeams which vanish

Beyond occlusions
A full moon waits   in cider
The orange slice   turns

Dark sky   gusts of wind
Carry off flurries   of leaves
From graveyard trees

The lawn   fireflies
The old man sits   head in hands
Crying silently

Dry maple leaves
Scurry over the sidewalk
With a snail's shell

Light

On the slender leaves
Backlit   mayfly shadows   some
Busy   some   at rest

From darkened boughs
Dew points depend   so slight
Each a moon of silver light

Carelessly flinging
The odd shaped stone   but it skips so well
On the autumn pond

Bowing   as does its reed
The reflection   still water
About to ripple

Redwing blackbird
Unsteady perch   a bending reed
The gust   tumbles him off

Reminders

> *Marks on a page*
> *Again   history continues*
> *When I disagree   with me*

> *Under these leaves*
> *All of these haiku   millions*
> *And millions of millions*

> *Now   upon this pad*
> *As I write   the creature*
> *Smaller than a period*

> *On frosted glass*
> *The bamboo shadows   wave*
> *Wind I cannot feel*

Bay to Breakers
Lithe girl   but her utility belt
Tubes, cords, packs   and wires

Packed sand   churned
By footprints   each holds a puddle
Hosts of sand flies

June   under the eaves
Of the abandoned school
A nestling   calls

Iced over bird bath
Blackbirds land   slip and peck,
Make a racket   leave

How to Haiku

This was made out of a collection of haiku each of which began with the phrase "haiku instructions." Rather than present them in that fashion I revised them into this single piece.

The very first idea
That's all there is

    Let everything go by
    Stream over rocks

Cut to the chase   home in
    But leave 'em guessing

Actions and reactions
      No actor nor (scene)

Something old … becomes new
  Blossoms … fall out of the blue

    Timelessness   of each time
    Infinity   now

Quiet, peace and humanity
All in proportion

    Never, never,   never
    Make the same mistake twice

Keep close to nouns and verbs
Ooops   again

    Imagine not, reflect not
    Mediate not – not not

Publication Credits

Pg 1, 2ⁿᵈ <u>Cast The Line</u>*, Leanfrog, Berkeley, CA* 1980
Pg 1, 3ʳᵈ <u>(i)n((s(i)gh)t) to;(r(io)t)</u>*, One Insight Press, SF, CA* 2015
Pg 1, 4ᵗʰ BAPC Annual Contest* 2016
Pg 1, 5ᵗʰ <u>Cast The Line</u>*, Leanfrog, Berkeley, CA* 1980

Pg 2, 1ˢᵗ BAPC Annual Contest 2016
Pg 2, 3ʳᵈ <u>Mariposa #18</u> *HPNC*, SF, CA* 2008
Pg 2, 5ᵗʰ Published via Nomadic Grounds Coffee 2015

Pg 4, 4ᵗʰ BAPC Annual Contest 2016

Pg 5, 2ⁿᵈ <u>In Twilight, The Rising Moon</u>*, Leanfrog, Berk., CA* 1980
Pg 5, 5ᵗʰ <u>(i)n((s(i)gh)t) to;(r(io)t)</u>*, One Insight Press, SF, CA* 2015

Pg 8, 1ˢᵗ Published via Nomadic Grounds Coffee 2015
     <u>Mariposa #1</u>*, HPNC, SF, CA* 1999
     BAPC Annual Contest 2016

Pg 8, 4ᵗʰ <u>Mariposa #14</u>*, HPNC, SF, CA* 2006

Pg 11, 1ˢᵗ <u>Ashai Haikusit Network</u> 2008

Pg 18, 2ⁿ <u>Mariposa #14</u>*, HPNC, SF, CA* 2006

Pg 19, 4⁵ʰ <u>Ashai Haikusit Network</u>
                         2008

Pg 22, 2ⁿᵈ <u>International Haiku Festa</u>*, 1ˢᵗ place* 2004

Pg 30, 1ˢᵗ <u>A Path to the Sea</u>*, Two Autumns Press, SF, CA* 1996
Pg 30, 4ᵗʰ <u>Mariposa #18</u>*, HPNC, SF, CA* 2008
     <u>(i)n((s(i)gh)t) to;(r(io)t)</u>*, One Insight Press, SF, CA* 2015

Pg 32,3rd <u>(i)n((s(i)gh)t) to;(r(io)t)</u>*, One Insight Press, SF, CA* 2015

Pg 33, 2ⁿᵈ <u>(i)n((s(i)gh)t) to;(r(io)t)</u>*, One Insight Press, SF, CA* 2015

** BAPC: Bay Area Poet's Coalition, an SF area poet organization*
** HPNC: Haiku Poets of Northern California, a regional group*

Pg 33, 2ⁿᵈ <u>Woodnotes</u>*, SF, CA* 1994
Pg 33, 3ʳᵈ <u>A Path to the Sea</u>*, Two Autumns Press, SF, CA* 1996
Pg 33, 4ᵗʰ <u>A Path to the Sea</u>*, Two Autumns Press, SF, CA* 1996

Pg 34, 2nd <u>Evergreen</u>, English Haiku   *1999*

Pg 38, 2nd <u>(i)n((s(i)gh)t) to;(r(io)t)</u>, One Insight Press, SF, CA   *2015*

Pg 39. 1^s <u>Mariposa #1</u>, HPNC, SF, CA   *1999*
     <u>(i)n((s(i)gh)t) to;(r(io)t)</u>, One Insight Press, SF, CA   *2015*

Pg 41, 5th <u>Dreams Wander On</u>   *2010*
     <u>Haiku on Death and Dying</u>   *2010*

Pg 42, 1st The Vancouver Cherry Blossom Festival, 1st plc.   *2006*

Pg 44, 1st <u>Cast The Line</u>, Leanfrog, Berkeley, CA   *1980*
Pg 44, 1st <u>Cast The Line</u>, Leanfrog, Berkeley, CA   *1980*

Pg 47, 1^{std} <u>(i)n((s(i)gh)t) to;(r(io)t)</u>, One Insight Press, SF,CA   *2015*

Pg 55, 2nd <u>In Twilight, The Rising Moon</u>, Leanfrog, Berk., CA   *1980*

Pg 49, 2nd <u>(i)n((s(i)gh)t) to;(r(io)t)</u>, One Insight Press, SF,CA   *2015*
Pg 49, 5th BAPC Annual Contest   *2016*

Pg 51, 1st <u>HPNC's Newsletter #18</u>, HPNC, SF, CA   *2000*
Pg 51, 5th <u>(i)n((s(i)gh)t) to;(r(io)t)</u>, One Insight Press, SF,CA   *2015*

Pg 52, 2nd <u>(i)n((s(i)gh)t) to;(r(io)t)</u>, One Insight Press, SF, CA   *2015*

Pg 56, 3rd <u>Woodnotes</u>, SF, CA   *1995*

Pg 60, 2nd <u>In Twilight, The Rising Moon</u>, Leanfrog, Berk., CA   *1980*

Pg 61, 3rd <u>Mariposa, Number 17</u>, HPNC, SF, CA   *2007*

Pg 65,2nd <u>Ko, 20th Anniversary Vol. 21 #4</u>   *2006*

Pg 69, 1st <u>A Path to the Sea</u>, Two Autumns Press, SF, CA   *1996*
     <u>Mariposa #12</u>, HPNC, SF, CA   *2005*

Pg 72, 1st <u>(i)n((s(i)gh)t) to;(r(io)t)</u>, One Insight Press, SF, CA   *2015*
Pg 72, 2nd <u>(i)n((s(i)gh)t) to;(r(io)t)</u>, One Insight Press, SF, CA   *2015*

Pg 75, 3rd <u>(i)n((s(i)gh)t) to;(r(io)t)</u>, One Insight Press, SF, CA   *2015*

Pg 86, 3rd <u>A Feather Floating on Water</u>, Anthology, SF, CA   *2013*

Pg 90, 2^{nd h} <u>(i)n((s(i)gh)t) to;(r(io)t)</u>, One Insight Press, SF, CA 2015

Yes! Give this book away!

When you give this book away, please initial and indicate where and when you handed it off. I'd like these books to meander the world over and perhaps migrate back to San Francisco someday as kind of message in a bottle. I look forward to its MUNI debut, finding at a garage sale or on a shelf in a used bookstore.

Initials	**City**	**Date**

Initials   **City**   **Date**

____

____

____

____

____

____

____

Once this page is full, please use any other page—go for it!